No Time To Choose

Michael D. White

DEDICATED

THIS BOOK IS DEDICATED TO ALL THE PEOPLE THAT GAVE ME THE COURAGE TO WRITE THIS .I COULD NOT HAVE DONE IT WITHOUT YOUR FRIENDSHIP AND SUPPORT. JUSTIN, ELLEN, TOMMY, JAMES, ANTHONY, HANK MALY, NANCY

In Memory:

STEPHANIE P DUPIN. I MISS YOU SO MUCH. I STILL CRY TO THIS DAY

More Books from Michael White

Wherever You Call Me

Too Late For Smiling

Comforting Hope

Welcome Home Ann

Breathe Into Being

Ascension Into Dreams

NO
TIME
TO
CHOOSE

Chapter 1

To say today has been one of the worst ones in a while would be a massive understatement!

After a day of feeling like everything's going wrong, I think I'm finally at my breaking point.

Of course the shelter sadly had no rooms free again this morning, which was expected.

Then I went to see Joseph, who owned the local bakery, hoping desperately that I could do some work for him since my cash had completely depleted, only to find the normally lively bakery closed.

Deciding to put off dealing with the painful hunger I was feeling at the time, I pushed forward and went over to the park.

Despite it being sunny it was also 15 degrees (Celsius) today, not many were there for me to help. One lady got me to walk her dog but that only landed me $5.00 towards the food I was really needing.

So here I am, so hungry that I feel like I could be sick and cold enough that my face is going numb. I endure the icey walk towards the soup kitchen in dire need of the warm food they offer.

Of course, my luck doesn't come back the moment I arrive there. Walking through the door I can see tables filled with others, and

I can't help but notice the line is non-existent as I go over to the counter.

"Hello. Could I please get a serving of soup please?" I ask politely, confusion slowly taking over my features when I see no food on display like normal.

"I'm sorry, we were overloaded due to the cold tonight. We don't have any hot food left." The young man informs me with a regretful look.

Hearing the pain in my stomach growl out between us, I decide to just nod his way and go by the shelter for warmth before heading to my bridge for the night.

As I'm walking through the doors I only just entered moments ago, the man from before runs over to me and grabs my shoulder from behind. The sudden contact makes me jump since I rarely have human contact. Giving me an apologetic look before clearing his throat awkwardly, he brings a fraction of light back into my night.

"Umm... We still have some bread rolls left. I know it's not much but would you like to have one?" He offers with a small smile, holding a roll in his hand towards me.

"Thanks." I say with a small smile, grateful I at least have something to put in my stomach now.

I walk out with my head hanging low, feeling defeated while I try to eat the first bit of food I've had all day. What do I do now? Where do I go? What did I do to anyone that the heavens had cursed me to this Existence in life . After crying my eyes out for what seemed like hours, I decided to get up. I knew I couldn't lay there for too long. Time and space doesn't wait for anyone and I knew it wasn't going to wait for me.I wasn't Ready to die I just wanted the pain to stop.

I was tired of crying, and I was tired of feeling sorry for myself. I had to get up and face the truth, and the truth was that I was homeless. After I cried for a while, and became angry for a while, and cried again, there was just no more crying left. In the leaving of my tears from my face, my soul left with them, And the only thing remaining was its empty shell.

Chapter 2

When I was a few blocks away from the shelter I saw a group of people near the alleyway up ahead. History has proven itself clear to avoid people on Friday nights, since people do stupid things while drinking with others.

Deciding it's probably best to go around the group, I go to the road and start to wait for a break in the busy traffic. As the traffic light changes to red, I look over to check the groups where about only to see them taunting a small boy who can't be more than 15.

The local idiots were calling out to him, taunting him down the alley. The light changes green and the traffic flows again, but I can't help the pull that tells me to keep an eye on how far they go.

Hearing the hurtful words and laughter continue, I quickly make my way closer without drawing attention. They have some nerve in them, to even start spitting on the poor kid who is clearly scared out of his mind by the giants around him.

I find my feet moving without my knowledge as I go closer to the group, deciding it's better I take their mess instead of this kid.

The moment one of them raises his hand to harm the shaking boy, I find my courage to interfere.

"Oi! Leave the kid alone!" I yell out, hoping to sound as fierce as I'm trying. Though by the drunken smile, I doubt it.

"Well well, well, what do we have here fellas?" He whistles while looking at his friends. "Perhaps you can replace him and get beat up.

I move closer to the group, making sure to stay in the kids' view. I keep my hands behind my back as I walk over so only he can see them and start to gently wave my hand to the side, signaling for him to leave.

"Sorry but I'm not interested. But there's a fight club right down the street I say as I see the kid shuffle his bum to the side.

"I'm not interested." I tell him to try to keep my distance from fear of being hurt or even worse killed.

As I saw the kid standing up and bolting down the street, I decided I needed to make a quick exit. The Boy kept his eyes on me the entire time.

Going for the most effective method to incapacitate a man, I lift my knee swiftly into his groin. The moment his hands let go to cup his surely aching balls, I turn to make a run for it.

Getting a whole two steps before hands grab me and slam me backwards to the floor. Groaning from the impact, I look up to see the other friends glaring at me.

The ball Boy stands with a beyond furious look aimed my way. I can't help but cower as much as possible, the man hovers with his friends with a sick smile upon his face.

"That wasn't very nice. Since you just took away one option of entertainment, you'll just have to make up for it." He chuckles before he pulls his leg back and lands a hard kick into my side.

I can't even pretend it doesn't hurt like hell, I'm skin and bone and they're brute muscle on a binge.

When I feel like I've recovered, his mates and him start to kick everywhere that's in front of them. Keeping my arms over my face, I curl into a ball trying to protect myself as much as I can. Feeling boots hit all over my legs and body, I can't help but be grateful they're not hitting my head.

"Get the hell away from him?!" A deep voice booms over the group making their actions hot.

"Who are you? Major Payne?" One slurs, laughing with his friends.

"I can be, if you want." The voice says before I hear the smack of impact and a loud groan that follows.

Looking up to see a muscular man that looked like he was straight out of the army, I can't help but feel relieved that he's here to help me and not them.

I see one of the Boys on his arse, holding his nose as it gushes blood. All of his friends quickly helped him up except for the prick that started all this. He looks ready to blow a fuse.

Not sure how this will all end, I shuffle my aching body backwards until I'm leaning against the alley wall. I suspect this is where I'll sleep tonight since moving is a painful process now.

"You're gonna pay for that!" He seethes before charging my savior.

Hearing another smack makes my curiosity spike, looking up to see the lead dickhead on the ground holding his stomach coughing.

"Now screw off and don't let me see you around here again." He tells them in a deathly calm tone that even scares me a little.

They scurry away with their injured friends so quickly you'd think they were never even there in the first place. With the immediate threat gone and my adrenalin slowed, the severe pain my body is in comes back full force.

"Was that her bud?" The deep voice questions as I close my eyes and try to slow my breathing down.

"Yeah." A small voice says before I feel a timit hand on mine.

Quickly opening my eyes to be greeted with the boy from earlier, I can't help but give him a small smile.

He's okay.

That was all that mattered.

"I got my friends to come as quickly as we could." He says quietly with a frown. "This is Eddy." The kid gestures to the giant man that saved me. "And this is Remy." He tells me, pointing to a Boy with long brown hair behind him. "And I'm Pat."

"Thanks kid. Are you okay?" I ask, hoping the group didn't scare him too much.

"I'm okay." He says sadly, while looking over at me. "I'm sorry we didn't get here sooner." He whispers.

"Hey. It's okay. You ended up saving me so we're square." I smile at him hoping to soothe his worries.

"Sir, do you have a place we can take you to? Maybe the hospital?" The giant known as Eddy offers.

"Thanks big Boy but I think I'll just stay here tonight." I give a weak smile, feeling exhaustion and hunger takes over.

Next thing I know I'm being lifted high into the air, letting out a squeak from shock and the pain. I look up to see Eddy holding me bridal style before I feel a small hand grasping mine. I relax knowing it's Pat and he is with me too.

Moments later we go into the familiar doors of the shelter. At first I thought they were just going to dump me here but then I heard the ladies at reception greet the Boys who came or helped me.

"Eddy, I didn't know you had a son." Rachel snickers at the big Boy.

"Not my son, but he could use the doc or a first aid kit." He tells them before walking through a door that looks like it leads to a lounge area.

Sitting me down gently, Pat doesn't drop my hand once. Feeling him sit next to me still, I give his hand a small squeeze to let him know I'm doing okay.

"Oh my goodness!! Jean is getting the doctor in right now. Michael what the hell happened?!" Rachel says as she grabs my face to make me look her way.

Seeing the worry is kind of nice, but all I want to do is sleep. I'm hungry, sore as hell and so damn tired.

"Some drunks started messing with Pat on his way home, he stepped in apparently. This is what they did before we got back to him." Eddy tells a sad looking Rachel.

"I got the doc Rach-" Jean walks in but halts her steps when she sees it's me. "Oh Michael," she gasps as her hands fly up to her mouth.

A woman walks in with what I'm guessing is a medical bag before she tells Eddy to take me to the nurses room for privacy. After being laid on the bed, she tells everyone to leave before she talks me through the examination.

"You got very lucky. Nothing appears broken, but you will be very sore. Some painkillers won't help with that though. I'd like to check you over again another day to check the healing of it all though." She says kindly to me, handing me a packet of Nurofen and some water.

After taking 2 tablets I decide it's best to leave, I really don't need the reminder of what I'm so desperately wanting.

Walking over to reception, I see the girls talking with Eddy and Pat. Though as soon as they see me their conversation dies off.

"Thanks for the help, I'm going to head out now. See you tomorrow girls." I say as I start to hobble away, I'm not really in the mood to be told the same thing as always.

"Wait! Michael, wait!" Jean shouts as she runs over to me. "We were hoping you'd come by today, but then you didn't show up." She tells me to draw my brows together in confusion.

"Umm. Sorry Jean..." Not really sure why she was telling me that.

"We wanted to tell you a bed opened up!" She practically squeals, making my breathing stop.

"W-what...?" I whisper.

This can't be right...

A room never opens up and when they do I'm always too late.

They had no beds free this morning.

"A bed in one of our rooms freed up after lunch today. We want to offer it to you!"

She smiles at me, looking so happy her face might split in half.

"U-umm..." I stutter quietly, feeling my breathing get shallow at the overwhelming sensation that's swiftly coursing through my veins.

"Michael, are you okay?" Rachel asks, walking towards us as black spots start to invade my vision.

"Yeah..." I mumble moments before the black spots quickly take over all of my sight and I feel like I'm falling.

"Michael"

Pat's shouting is the last thing I hear before I finally slip into unconsciousness. Hearing faint noises nearby, my brain tries to comprehend where I must be. I'm warm, which is the first thing that makes me question exactly where my location is, as well laying on something really soft compared to the sleeping bag I normally use. Yesterday's events are still a little fuzzy.

Finally opening my eyes to be greeted by a small sized room painted cream that had another bed on the opposite wall, a set of side drawers and tall boys next to each other.

Although a room had become available at

the shelter I was still new to being

homeless, I didn’t know where to go before this shelter and I didn't know what to do. I wasn't sure where to go get food, how to take a shower, or where I would even sleep. I don't think I cared very much, I don't think I cared at all. Ultimately I sucked up the courage to ask someone if there were places I could go for any type of assistance. A few people were nice enough to show me around, and guide me to the right facilities.

I'm sure I looked strange in most people's eyes, because I was young, and the hair on my face hadn't even started growing, standing in line with his three-piece suit on, looking like a million dollar man. Some say looks can be deceiving, and if you saw me that day, you would have swore they were right. I was no more than a hundred and ten pounds soaking wet.

During the day, when I couldn't find somewhere to sleep, I walked for what seemed like miles. I never thought that, at the age of 19 or 20 I would be walking the streets of Los Angeles, homeless with dress shoes on. My toes began to shrivel up, like the Wicked Witch of the West, from The Wizard of Oz, when Dorothy landed her house on her. I desperately needed some shoes,walking shoes, because these dress shoes were almost worn to the sole. So I went into a shelter, since they allowed people to come in and shower, I received a change of clothes and some decent enough looking shoes.

Food started to be readily available, at any shelter I went to too. Remarkably, to have breakfast, I went to one shelter, then lunch at another, then dinner at a totally different shelter. I knew all the local shelter schedules in the area, and had no problem finding them. I decided since I was going to be down here for a while I would look for a job. I didn't know where to look, and I didn't know where to start looking. Transportation money was hard to come by, and nobody just gave out bus tokens for free. Luckily I was dressed decently enough, a van pulled alongside me while I was hurrying to make it to the final call for lunch.

Whoever was driving the van, seemingly didn't belong in the area, because they were dressed too nicely for that. The window rolled down, and a voice from the driver's seat said " Hey are you looking for a job?. That was the first time I had ever been approached by anybody asking for anything, but I was eager to see what the job was. So with excitement in my voice I asked myself what the job was about.

He began by telling me that he had a body to pick up, and I could join him if I was really serious about working. I wasn't too fond of jumping in people's cars, because God knows, it could have been Jeffrey Dahmer or another Richard Ramirez, behind the wheel. But I'm sure I could have protected myself if need be. I wasn't quite sure what he meant by "body to pick up" and it didn't sound like he was a part of any taxi service I knew of.

So he pulled over and I hesitantly jumped into the van. Still leery and apprehensive about some random Boy just pulling over and asking anybody if they needed a job. But I figured if you were that bold, you must have been desperately looking for someone to help you. and luckily I was desperately looking for a job. Right away he explained what he did, and I was extremely excited. He was a funeral director for one of the largest funeral homes in Southern California.

I've never worked with dead bodies, and the only one I have ever seen was at a funeral. I'm sure the experience was going to be something that I would never forget. We arrived at our destination, which was a residential house, where someone had passed away, and our job was to remove the body. So I jumped out of the van, and we both went to the back to grab the cart. I thought I'd be more afraid walking into the house, and knowing that there was a dead body waiting for me, but I wasn't afraid at all. To be honest, I was more intrigued than anything, because the thing I had wished for, prayed for, and desired with every fiber of my being, was there staring me in the face.

I was now in this room, with the funeral director, and a dead body. I was looking death directly in the eyes, and it was cold. The person had died of a heart attack in their sleep. And was found by a relative the next morning. At that moment I couldn't tell you what I was thinking, but I knew what I was looking at, and what I was looking at was not something I wanted. The person's body had become filled with rigamortis and stiffness, trying to get them out of the bed, seemed like it was going to be an insurmountable task but we did it.

We slowly made our way out of the house, trying our best not to hit anything as we left. I could still hear the families, cries and screams as we slowly closed the door on their family members forever. I couldn't imagine what they felt knowing that was the last time you were going to see your family member in that house. I'm sure it must have been painful. I'm sure that was an image they were never going to be able to forget about. As we pulled off I quietly said a prayer for the family, and for the family member we were about to take to the funeral home.

In that surreal moment, I forgot about my problems, I forgot about the fact that I was homeless, and I forgot about the fact that I didn't have a place to stay. Despite all that, it wasn't about me anymore, it wasn't about my problems, and my issues, I had found my niche . Everyday we would meet at the same place & time then head out to do the pickup or drop offs. Nevertheless it was time for me to go to the next step of the job which included preparation of the remains for funerals.

By this time, I'd seen everything there was to see, as far as death but this was totally different. This was up close and personal. There were moments of sheer terror thinking the bodies were going to sit up and start talking,but my fears were overcome fairly quickly due to the Process one had to go through. Nothing and I mean nothing could have prepared me for being homeless. Nothing I had ever seen or done had prepared me for this type of pain. This type of pain only came from the deepest and darkest of places. But nothing came close to the pain when I had to stop pretending and finally and honestly admitted to myself that I was homeless..

No one ever wants to hear someone say those words. Especially not coming from your own mouth. You would be better off saying, "You had killed someone" over saying you were homeless. I couldn't lie to myself anymore. The truth was out.

My daily routine was set in stone, breakfast at the union rescue mission, lunch at Los Angeles mission,and dinner at the Salvation Army. I had a change of clothes daily,which included a shower and a hygiene kit and all the clean socks and underwear I could use. The four block areas of skid row was my dwelling place and I dared not venture outside of that, because I just couldn't face people being homeless.

In the funeral business, the only people that needed to see you were the dead and their families but to wonder outside of that would be considered blasphemous. It was easy to forget about all the problems you had working in a funeral home. The atmosphere wasn't conducive to anything other than that in which you were working at that time. Everyday there was something new to learn and experience,so taking the time out to cry was absolutely out of the question.

I worked 7 days a week just so I didn't have to think about the circumstances I was in. Working kept my mind off being homeless. The only time I would think about it, was at night,when I had to find somewhere to sleep.

Sleeping didn't come easily as I had anticipated. There was always something going on,from the many police and fire trucks going down the street, to the stray cats and dogs mating or fighting next to me when I had a safe place to sleep.

It was always interrupted by Junkie's trying to get their fix and before I knew it morning had arrived. The shelters started to be very strict on who they allow to shower, get a change of clothes, and even eat.

They wanted you to join their program, that was technically for drugs and alcohol rehabilitation, then they would render their services. Anyone else was just out of luck. Since drugs and alcohol wasn't my vice. I didn't feel any need to join their program.

So I continued to do my daily routine, until I wasn't allowed to any longer. I had become delegated to taking one shower a week, as well as one change of clothes,and I could only eat there every other day.

Tuesdays at most shelters were in my eyes sightseeing days. It seemed like everyone volunteered that day .

They would feed the homeless, ask questions that only nosy people ask,and take pictures, like everyone was at an amusement park. I hated Tuesdays. It was bad enough that I was homeless, but I didn’t quite accept it, and the last thing I wanted to do was be seen by someone I knew.

Unfortunately for me, someone had changed the schedule and didn't give me the memo, because the day that I was signed up was the day that the volunteers were there.

CHAPTER 3

Too Ashamed To Die

I decided to come on a Friday instead of my normal day, which was a Wednesday. And like I said before, volunteers would only be there on Tuesday. I went without a shower for at least three days, and the clothes that I had on, started to turn brown. I was working so much that I forgot to do anything hygienically, so as you could already imagine I was a little tart.

So I stood in line,waiting to get my tray for breakfast. Not really thinking about anyone or anything. To my surprise, the girl that I had taken to my high school prom was one of the volunteers ,and the one passing out the trays. In that instant she called my name, with a look of disgust, and ill repute, written all over her face. She asked me " What was I doing there"? "And why am I in line waiting on a tray"? I calmly said "Because I'm homeless and I need to eat" Without saying a word her voice rose in anger, And she hollered loudly "HOMELESS ARE YOU KIDDING ME".

I was beyond embarrassed, and by that time,I lost my appetite completely and ran out of line.

I couldn't go back, I couldn't go back to that place, no matter what I did, and no matter what I said, I just couldn't go back there. The One person I thought would understand any situation, including my situation, would understand why I was there, and would have some type of heart.

But I was wrong. If you wanted me dead at that moment, you just got your wish.

There was nothing left of me. everything inside of me, died in that moment. I died at that moment. My heart died at that moment. I didn't want to work, I didn't want to eat. I just wanted to die. I wanted to jump out in front of a car, and pray that one-hit would be it. I wanted to take a knife and slit my wrists, until the blood had escaped my body. I never went back to the funeral home again, because I didn't want to work there, I wanted to be in the casket, while someone was working on me.

There was nothing left to cry about, because I just didn't feel any pain. Everything that gave me the desire to live, now's given me the desire to die. It wasn't what she said, it was how she said it. I didn't ask to be homeless, and I certainly didn't ask to live here. Before I knew it, the tears had engulfed my soul, broke open my spirit, and unleashed a Title Wave of emotions. They're on that ground, where urine and feces lay prostrate and inert. Where the streets were littered with needles, from the junkies that pushed them in their arms. Where the dirt is undyed and unchanged. There on that cold ground,that smelled of rot and disease. My soul opened up.

My heart opened up for all the world to see. For all the days, all the ways and for all the times I had disobeyed, disrespected, and Delusioned mySELF from myself. My heart lay there on that ground and cried. Not because I wanted it too, or because it needed too, but because I had neglected it, when it needed me the most. They're on that ground, on that Hallowed Ground, my heart opened up. And when it completely opened itself, and poured out all that it had to pour out, It wasn't completely finished because it poured out some more. There I was a puddle of the person I used to be, there I was laying on the ground waiting to die, there on that ground lay a homeless version of myself, and the person looking back at me was not me.

Was this the end? Was this where my life was going to end? Was this the place that I wanted to end it at? And with each question the answer always came back the same. The answer always came back silent, silent because no one was doing the talking, and no one was doing the asking.

How could one’s life end if no one was willing to end it. Although I knew in my heart I didn't want to die, I didn't want to cry either. I didn't want to feel the pain that I was feeling, nor did I want to embrace it. Maybe I needed to go? Maybe I needed to get away?. Maybe I needed to go find that person that was looking back at me?.

Maybe just maybe I needed to go find me.

CHAPTER 4

Finding Me

I was tired of all the crying, and I just couldn't lay on the ground and continue dying. I needed to get up so I made a decision to move on. There was nothing left for me where I was, only the shadow of myself. So with the last remaining money in my pocket, I went to the Greyhound bus station, where I bought a one-way ticket to Texas. I didn't know where I was going, nor did I know exactly how to get there, but I knew I couldn't be here.

So I hopped on that bus, and waved goodbye to California. I arrived in Texas, later than I expected to the next morning. I was still homeless but at least I wasn't homeless in California. I started to ask questions and make friends. I didn't know whether these people were good or bad but I knew something had to be better than where I came from. I connected with a group of people on that bus, and we all just so happen to be traveling looking for something better. Better didn't come easy in fact I spent days begging for spare change on the side of the road.

Chapter 5

I drag my hand across the cold old bricks of a building covered in graffiti. It had been years from what I was told since the building shut down due to unknown reasons. I had been living near it for about—3 years or so. As strange as it may seem, it was the only thing that remained the same throughout my stay.

As I neared the end of its rainbow art bricks, I found myself back on the sidewalk of an empty street. But what did I expect at 3 Am. Everyone had houses and apartments to go home to, food to eat, nice warm beds to sleep in. What did I have? A makeshift box in which I had taken a few other boxes and pieced them together with old chewed up gum.

When it would rain the box would leak, and sag. I had to find sticks at the park to prop it up from time to time.

It wasn't the most ideal place to sleep, but it kept me off of benches and out of doorways.

The street was silent besides the few vehicles that would drive by and splash water onto the sidewalk. I walked to a nearby bus stop in hopes to sit for a while before continuing on to the dumpsters of Pizza Hut.

Every day, in the early morning, I would take the backstreet of the graffiti-covered building and head down to Frost street to

Pizza Hut's dumpsters. They typically would end up having a ton of leftovers—or trashed food— for me to dig out.

I reached the bus stop only to find an older man, gray beard, dark skin, and awfully thin sleeping on it.

I guess I'll just sit on the ground.

I sat down and watched as the traffic slowly picked up.

People would be getting up for work soon.

Me and the other people aren't so different, we both sleep, eat, dream, and even work. The only thing is my work and their work is different. I worked to survive, even if it meant eating food out of the dumpsters with the rats.

From time to time, a nice old couple would give me a few dollars here and there. They never questioned what I did with it either. People like that have always given me hope that there are still good, unselfish people in the world.

But other times,

I would be given smug looks from strangers passing when I would ask for a dollar or so, so I could purAnthony some toiletries

But could I blame them for not wanting to hand over their hard earned money to some street rat like me?

I suppose I couldn't. I probably wouldn't either if I haven't lived like them or had their experiences.

I'm just a sketchy young adult named Michael, who would want to help a street rat like me?

Chapter 7

I sat there at the bus stop for a while until I began to see the sunrise, that's how I knew it was for sure safe to head to the dumpsters. I stood and dusted my already dirty jeans off and took another glance at the man. He was awake now and in a somewhat daze. I waved my hand in front of his face, I saw him before and actually spoke with him before as well.

He told me that he had returned from the military and lost his job. He had no family nearby, only his wife—who passed away two weeks after he returned. Now there he is, on a bench of a bus stop. A man who served this country tossed aside.

"Michael," he said as he looked up at my dirty face, " my, you are getting taller by the day." He smiled an almost toothless smile. He grew to become more like a father to me, or a grandpa even. I sat beside him and gave him a hug, "Thanks, Mr. Lawson."

"Have you found any food yet?" He asked. Though me and him both were in the same boat, he never sought for him, he only worried about me.

I shook my head, "no sir, not yet. I'm about to go to the dumpsters and find something."

He shook his head and shoved his hand into his old, raggedy coat pocket, "No young lady like you is gonna be digging in the dumpster when," he pulled out a Kellogg's Protein Bar, "when I have something that isn't trash, here." He held it out for me.

My eyes gazed upon it. It wasn't often I got to see an unopened thing of food. It was like heaven to behold it.

As much as I wanted to accept, I declined, "No, no," he gently pushed his hand back to him, "that's yours, you need it." I gave him a gentle smile.

"Michael," he said somewhat seriously, "I am not but an old man, my time here is little. But you, your years should be long—you take this and fill yourself." He placed the bar in my lap and rose to his feet, balancing himself with his makeshift cane, "I will see you around the youngster. Take care of yourself." He walked off.

So kind... so unselfish.

I ate the protein bar and it calmed my raging stomach. After the sun had risen a bit more, I ended up on the corner of the street holding my sign that said 'Money for food.' To many, it would be an embarrassment and even public display of devastation. However, to me, it was a means of survival.

Many people don't give their money to street rats like me because they fear and assume we will buy drugs or cigarettes with it. So, my thought was that if I would display what exactly I would use the money for, they would be more considerate.

As the clock shifted from 6:59 to 7 o'clock, the street began to get busier. People passed by me and read the sign, but no luck. They continued by talking on their cell phones or texting or just flat out ignoring me.

Come on

I thought as I sat with my legs crossed.

Being a teen on the street was one of the most difficult things.

When our stomach would growl from the lack of food we had to find it in any way we could. We had to compensate in any way we could.

After an hour or so had passed, a girl, about my age, handed out $10.

"I usually don't do this stuff, but— I know dealing with Aunt Flo when you have money can be difficult, much more when you don't," I took the 10 and smiled.

"Thank you so much," I said as she walked off.

Great! Now I can buy food and stuff!

I was overjoyed by the girl's generosity and kindness.

Many don't realize that it's hard being a teen Especially on the streets.

Chapter 8

I walked to the nearest convenience store that carried more than just packets of sunflower seeds and condoms. I walked into the brightly lit store and the store clerk whipped his head around at me. His stubble covered face that was fixed into an angry expression. As I roamed around the store to find anything I could eat other than snacks, he kept his eyes on me. As if I were some sort of criminal.

But that was to be expected when a store clerk sees a ratty, dirty teen like me. A lot of street kids don't have good reputations, I was just one of the ones who kept their morals.

I skimmed the shelves and my eyes laid on a loft of bread and some tuna in a can. I stood on my tiptoes to reach it but failed. I looked around and the store clerk still had those fixated eyes. I pursed my lips and looked back at the bread that was out of my reach.

Should I ask for help?

I glanced back at him, his expression seemed to grow even more suspicious of my presents being there.

I hesitated and tried again, still couldn't reach it.

At that point I figured it would be useless for me to continue to look like an idiot.

I shrugged and walked to the front where the clerk didn't let up on his cold looks.

"Excuse me sir, can you—"

"Give you that bread for free? No, I can not and will not. Now scram kid." His voice was cold and harsh.

I furrowed my brows and slapped the $10 on the counter. I wasn't about to leave that store without that bread and tuna.

"I have money to pay for it so listen before you assume," with that I walked back to the back of the store and pointed at the bread that I needed.

"Those," I stood on my tip toes.

He gave me a smug look before going back there and retrieving loft of bread and tuna "Anything else," he mumbled.

The bread cost $2, and the tune was $2 . I had 6 left. I looked around and my eyes fell on a $1 bottle of Tylenol . I went to grab the bottle when the clerk grabbed my wrist, "No Sir."

I spun my head around and looked him dead in the eyes, "What do you mean 'no'?"

"I know what kids like you do with that stuff."

"Use it for pain?"

"No, you pop 'em like its candy."

I was furious at that point and I let my hand fall to my side.

We stood there as I kept my eyes focused on the medicine. I knew I would need it and would be in a lot of pain without it. Thoughts filled my head of ways to get it without the clerk knowing, but as I said before, I was the one street kid who had some morals to 'em.

I sighed and started toward the front with the clerk not far behind me.

I wasn't about to compromise my morals for a little pain medicine.

He set the bread and tuna on the counter and began to ring it up when my eyes caught a glimpse of what seemed like heaven.

A small warmer of those huge, soft pretzels. I licked my lips and scanned for the price of them.

$4

It was rather expensive, but it would be getting cold soon. According to the weather in a thrown away newspaper, it was supposed to get into the 40's that coming night and I knew I would probably need something warm to keep my insides from freezing.

I pushed my hunger and thoughts aside and just settled with the bread and tuna. There was no use in buying the pretzel then anyways, it would just get cold before nightfall

Chapter 9

After I left the store I went and sat at the park on an old wooden bench. I sat in the box that was covered in a bag next to me while I just admired some of the families there.

I watched as a father and his little girl crossed the grass. Her warm smile was followed by giggles as he caught her and spun her around.

I wonder if my mom did that with me..

My mother gave me up to foster care when I was only 1 ½ years old, since then I was just getting by the easiest way possible. Many times I would be left at the house with my other siblings to fend for ourselves for days on end.

I could hardly remember what my mother even looked like. Did she have black hair like the lady with the newborn baby by the water fountain? Or did she have chestnut brown like the lady near the swing sets?

Everything was blurry, I suppose it was because I was so young.

The little boy and her father returned to her mother and his wife. They seemed so happy.

That was something I missed most, happiness. I wasn't sure what it even felt like anymore.

I sat there for what felt like forever but was actually 3 hours. It was then that a park patrol officer came passing by and stopped in front of me.

"Sir I am gonna have to ask you to move," he said to me as he hooked his thumbs in his belt loop.

I looked up at him, "This is a public park,"

"Well there are people who want to sit and you have been here for almost 4 hours."

I wasn't about to move just because I had been there for a while. It was a public place and nobody owned that bench. I remained seated.

"No," I said bluntly.

"Excuse me?"

" I said no."

Right then I felt a gut wrenching feeling as he narrowed his eyes at me.

"Listen here, you have been there for one hour too long. There are families who are sitting on the grass—not voluntarily—but because there's nowhere to sit," he pointed at a nearby family of four, "this place is open to the public for enjoyment, not a housing space for street rats like you." And with that he grabbed me up by my arm and sent me on my way.

I didn't return to that park...

Chapter 10

Once I left that park I headed downtown where a group of street rats like me gathered. They'd gather there and sometimes trade stuff such as clothes, or food and sometimes even drugs and alcohol.

I would typically go and trade off any little piece of wood I would find in a dumpster in return for articles of clothing or some other sort of food. Over 99% of the time, most of the teens would trade unfairly to those who were starving and such.

Once, I saw a man trade his last piece of clothing for a bite size piece of bread. The man roamed the backstreets nude until one day he was found dead behind the courthouse. Some say he was killed while others were led to believe it was a natural death.

Both are possibilities when living on the streets but everyone knew good and well why he died.

It was during the winter and the temperatures were dropping below 40° every night. With him out there naked, it was only a matter of time before he succumbed to the cold. The ambulance went and retrieved his body and us street rats were left with not even a word of what exactly was the cause of his death.

Therefore we just assumed.

As I approached the group I noticed a familiar face.

Anthony.

As I drew closer to the group he whipped his head around and his brown eyes met my eyes. He was also a street rat as they would call it. Although he'd been on the street longer than I had, he was making due pretty well. He had full articles of clothing, even a dodgers cap. He managed to find a pair of almost new Nikes in an apartment store dumpster along with some weight lifting gloves that he'd only wear because they looked cool.

"Well if it isn't O'l Michael," his surprisingly white teeth always made me envious when I saw them. How could someone live on the street and have that perfect of teeth.

"Hey Anthony," there I was, standing next to Anthony along with the group. Everyone was exchanging clothes, drugs and food. As I watched I noticed a rather nice flannel float from hand to hand. I wanted it.

I guess I started a bit too long and someone took notice of it.

"You want it?" A grungy girl asked me as she passed it my way. I held the flannel in my hands for a little while. Observing it; it was my size, favorite color, and it would have kept me warm through the cold nights ahead. I looked up at the girl whose eyes were fixated on me and the flannel, "What would you want for it?"

"Some food and maybe," a devilish, perverted grin appeared on her face, "something more?"

My once smile quickly faded to a disgusted frown as I threw the flannel at her, "Heck no! You pervert!" Anthony snapped his head around to see me utterly disgusted.

He perked an eyebrow, "What-What happened?" He questioned.

It wasn't uncommon for people—male and female—to ask for sexual things during the trades. That's how many of them got STD's and such.

I wasn't about to sell myself out for a flannel. That girl could have AIDS, HIV, Mono, who knows.

"I'm just gonna leave now, there's nothing good anyways." I turned and started to leave when Anthony grabbed my arm.

"Wait,"

"What?"

"Have you eaten yet?"

As I said before, he'd been on the street longer than I had. Which means he knew of all the ins and outs of getting half decent food that wasn't from a dumpster.

"A small protein bar." I murmured, letting my eyes drop to the ground.

"We are going to get you some real food!" He chirped.

"Real food?"

"Yep!"

"How are you going to do that?"

"Never doubt me, Michael." He gave me a small smile and we continued on.

That moment I took a mental note: Never doubt Anthony.

Chapter 11

Anthony led me down to an older Chinese fast food stand that was located about 2 or 3 miles from the group.

"Here we are," he said as he gazed up at a neon sign above the stand.

The place looked rather sketchy, but my stomach didn't care what the place looked like as long as it had real food.

"What would you like?"

My eyes gazed at the menu. I had no idea what any of it was, much less what it tasted like.

Orange Boyen?

The thought of it didn't seem too appetizing. I bit my lip and continued to look as I felt Anthony's eyes land on me.

"You don't know what you like, do you?"

I supposed he could tell by my confused and lost expression as I tried to make out the names of the food in my mind and word it out with my lips.

"The General Boyen is good. It comes with rice and an egg roll too. Um," I watched his eyes scan the menu like I did moments before, "and the orange Boyen is probably my favorite. It's somewhat sweet and it comes with two egg rolls and a little bit of rice."

"I'll take that."

"The orange Boyen?"

I wasn't sure exactly what it was, but I was sure it had to be somewhat decent for Anthony to like it. Never doubt Anthony..

He walked up to the counter of the stand and looked up at an Asian man, "Hey Rick!" He grinned.

The man returned the grin, "Hey Anthony, what can I get for you today?"

I was slightly surprised that the two were on a first name basis. Especially since I had a feeling Anthony mooched off of the dude.

"Well I would like to get some food for my friend here," he motioned for me to move closer. I stayed still.

Friend...

"Ahh, I see, I see. For the little Boy huh? What would you like to get?"

"The number four."

"Coming right up!" The Asian man turned and began fixing the food.

I kept my eyes locked on the dirty pavement as Anthony waited for the order to be complete. I was just amazed how Anthony didn't have to pay the man for it. Minutes passed and the man handed Anthony the food, "There you go Anthony!"

"Thanks Rick."

We waved goodbye to the man and started to walk once again. I wasn't sure where I was heading, but I knew Anthony knew.

"You're going to love this," he said as he led me into an alleyway, "it's sweet yet somewhat savory." He slipped the carryout bag over his arm and began to climb a ladder. I followed close behind despite my fear of heights.

I always had a terrible fear of heights. I had been that way since I was young.

My foster mother told me it was because I nearly fell out of my crib several times—but others had told me differently.

My old neighbor that lived next door to me when I was 5, told me that my foster mother held me over the balcony when she was trying to be mean.

The neighbor retrieved me and kept me in her place for the rest of that night.

We neared the top in only a matter of seconds. Anthony led me to the edge of the roof and sat down and dangled his feet over the edge. He sat the carryout bag down next to him and gazed out at the city. I sat beside him and looked out at it as well. It wasn't the most modern city one could live in, nor was it the nicest. It was full of gang activity; shootings, drug deals, sex trafficking. The whole nine yards.

"Do you ever look at this and wonder if you can ever escape it?" He asked me.

I glanced at him surprised by the questions and then looked down at my dirty jeans, "sometimes."

"Nothing good ever comes out being a street kid here."

All of that surprised me. Anthony was usually a positive soul, one who would look at the best in all things. But right then, he seemed like the saddest person I ever met.

"There's some truth in that, but—" we both glanced at the bag.

"You can eat—it is yours after all."

"Aren't you hungry?"

"I can get food there anytime... you eat."

He pushed it to me.

I opened it up and held the package of Boyen in my hands. It was warm, really warm. I opened it up and took a bite of the white meat Boyen. It was very sweet, just like he described earlier.

"But?" He questioned my earlier cut off.

"But—we don't have to be a part of the stereotypes."

We stayed silent for the rest of the time I ate. I finished everything. From the Boyen to the egg rolls and finished it off with the rice. Every wrapper fell onto the street below. They blew with the wind and trailed off to the shadows.

"Michael, I know you have a positive outlook most of the time. But sometimes you have to set it aside and look at reality."

What's he saying?

"We are like wrappers, we're here for a short amount of time. Only a few take notice. But like the wind, we will one day blow away." He stood and left me alone.

Chapter 13

As the evening drew nearer, the wind grew more chill. I decided to head back to the convenience store to buy myself one of those big pretzels that I had seen earlier. It made my mouth water thinking of just the warmth of it.

Though I had just eaten, I was still hungry. It had been 3 days since my last meal before I had eaten that protein bar.

It still surprised me what a person would do for a little food.

I walked a while and then rounded the corner that led to the convenience store. The night began to fall quickly as I drew closer. I didn't like being out of my box during the night. There was too many creeps looking for someone to take advantage of and such to satisfy their sexual desires.

I picked up my pace once I passed a rather dark man that gave me a mean glare.

I reached the store and swung the door open as I walked in.

There was a different store clerk that time.

Tylenol.

Was my only thought right then and there as I felt slight pain in my lower abdominal area. I bit my lip and headed to the back of the store where I was about to grab a bottle of ibuprofen.

I grabbed the bottle and headed to the front. If being pain free meant I would be a little hungry and cold for the night, it would be worth it.

I placed the bottle on the counter with the utmost of confidence. The lady looked at me and then the bottle. Her look was filled with suspicion, in which I assumed it was because of my appearance.

My eyes landed on the pretzels once again as she scanned the bottle of medicine and told me the amount to be paid. I wanted one so bad. I could taste the salt on my tastebuds and the warmth in my mouth. My stomach begged for it and yet my body begged for medicine. If I were to get the pretzel I wouldn't be able to get the medicine. And vice versa.

"Hello? Kid, that'll be two dollars."

I snapped back into reality and grabbed my left over five dollar bill.

So hungry...

I handed her the money as she popped open the register and started counting my cash back.

She glanced up at me once again and caught me staring at the pretzels.

"Are you hungry?"

I bit my lip and shook my head. I lied.

I hated pity, even though I really wanted that pretzel.

She gave me a smile of sympathy.

"I know you're homeless,"

Is it that noticeable?

"I was in here when Sam gave you a hard time this morning, I'm terribly sorry for that." She handed me my change.

"It's alright. I get it a lot."

As I said before, it wasn't anything new to be given dirty looks and denied service in stores and such.

"You shouldn't. There are a lot of dishonest homeless people but there's also a lot of dishonest people who aren't homeless,"

I hate that word...homeless...

"It doesn't mean he should assume you're going to use these the wrong way," she bagged the medicine and handed it over to me.

"Listen, I'm Amy. I'm the manager here. If you ever need anything, don't hesitate to ask." She leaned over the counter and motioned me closer, "I have been in your situation before. I know what it's like. I may not have been your age at the time but I know it's even harder. If you want one of those," she nodded toward the warm, salty pretzels, "You can have as many as you want. Just ask." With that, she stood upright again and smiled.

"What shifts do you work?" I asked.

"I work all week except Sundays after four PM."

"I'll come by tomorrow then," I turned and walked out.

The cold breeze hit my face as if someone slapped me with their hand. It was certain that winter was getting closer.

Another cold night to endure.

Chapter 14

I returned to my box just before 8 pm. It was dangerous to be out past that time, due to the son being completely down. I closed myself within the box and curled up. The sound of traffic began to fade as time ticked by. Only the sounds of people talking were left. From time to time I would hear someone walk back. Other times I would hear a dog whining and calling for its lost owner.

At least I had a box to go home to, unlike that mutt. The dog remained in the alleyway that my box housed on for several hours. It barked and howled nonstop, and kept me awake. I finally decided to open my makeshift doors on the box and peek out. When I did, I saw a small German Shepard puppy.

It perked its ears when it heard my box doors scrape across the pavement. It turned its head to me, and barreled at me.

Before I knew it and could close my doors, it was in the box with me.

I tried to push it out, but it kept coming back. It would scratch at my box and even managed to make a hole in it. I gave up trying to make it go away so I took it in.

The mutt and I eventually fell asleep and was awoken by the sound of thunder and a solid drip of water that repeatedly fell onto us. I shrugged and cursed under my breath and I scurried to find a stick to hold up the box top.

Once I found one, I propped it up and sat cross legged. The mutt remained in the same spot it was until light struck. It jumped up and hopped in my lap as if I was its mother. It whimpered in my arms as I tried to calm it.

How could someone just leave you all alone... you're so sweet, and calm natured. I couldn't understand why someone would just abandon the pup. You could tell it wasn't too old, and you could tell it was well taken care of. I tried to make myself believe that someone forgot him by accident, but I wasn't that naive.

We sat there while the rain continued to saturate the box. It would be only a matter of time before the box finally gave in. But to our surprise, it didn't. The rain stopped and the sound of tires splashing through the water was audible. I peeked out the box to see puddles all around my home, and that some of the street lights had lost power. Everything was dark. A chill ran down my spine as my clothes were soaked from water drops that had dripped in.

The mutt continued to whimper as I sat it aside and climbed out of the box.

From what I could see, it was nearly through. If another storm came, I would be covered in a blanket of wet cardboard.

I shrugged and knelt down to retrieve the mutt.

As I stood with him in my arms, I walked toward the exit of the alleyway. Toward the only street lamp that was on that I could see.

Once I reached the lamp, I slid down and leaned against it. The mutt licked my face a few times before laying his head down and going to sleep.

That was all I wanted to do—sleep.

But if I didn't stay awake and alert, I would most likely have woken up in a place that I didn't want to.

So much for a home...

Chapter 15

The hours dragged on and I could feel the cold seeping through my clothes even more. The night was long, and the temperature continued to drop. I watched the mutt sleep on my lap and I could see its breath in the cold.

I wish I had a coat like you do boy...

On the streets, even the animals had it better than we did. Everyone loved a good animal, everyone had pity on an animal. On a human? Not so much..

They assumed that we must have just been lazy, or brats that ran away. In many cases there were such things, however I just wished people wouldn't have assumed that with every person they saw on the streets.

I remained sitting for another hour before I noticed a drunken man that was heading my way. His steps were wobbly and his singing was slurred. I felt an uneasy feeling in my stomach however I had just started to feel slight warmth—or was it just my body adjusting to the cold?

I watched as he got closer and he leaned up against another nearby street lamp post.

"Well hi there boy," he said with a slurred voice. He'd obviously had drank too much at one of the bars. I ignored him and acted as if he wasn't even there.

"Hey, I'm talking to you," he shifted his weight from one foot to the other, "what's ur name?"

I kept my eyes on the mutt and refused to speak. Nothing good had come from slime balls like him. I bit my lip and stayed silent.

"Hey!" His voice boomed through the night. Not only did it startle me, but it startled the mutt as well. I looked up at the man, his coat hung off one shoulder and he held a cigarette in between his fingers.

"What's ur name?" He slurred once again. "Michael," I mumbled. I knew I should have remained silent, but he would have just kept yelling until I answered him. "Oh what a gorgeous little dog," he hiccuped and snickered, "—name. Such a lovely color too." I couldn't stop a blush flush onto my face when he said 'gorgeous.' I couldn't remember the last time I had a stranger call me that—or if one ever did.

"Thanks."

What does this Boy want from me?

I could feel the uneasy feeling begin to grow from within me. Yet, I didn't want to move. I didn't want him to think I was afraid of him.

Kill or be killed is how it had always been on the streets, and would forever be kill or be killed.

"I said I'm good," I snapped.

He perked an eyebrow and smirked. I stared across the street at a sign that read 'eggs and bacon! $1 between 9Am and 10Am.' It looked appetizing. I glanced back at the dude, who had moved three steps closer. I gasped and nearly fell over.

"Don't be startled boy," he placed a hand on my shoulder. My eyes stared at his clean hands. I wasn't expecting him to be so clean cut too.

"Don't touch me," I hissed and slapped his hand off.

He pursed his lips and smirked, "Oh, feisty are we?" He grabbed me up by my arm and I was on my feet.

I gritted my teeth and tried to get loose from his grip as the mutt started, confused. "Let go of me!" I shouted at the man. He grabbed my other arm and leaned close to my ear. I could feel his warm breath against my neck and I tensed up more. "I ain't gonna hurt you, I'm just going to make you feel really good— I'll even pay you." I couldn't believe what the man was offering. And as desperate and hungry and cold as I may have been, I wasn't that desperate.

"Let.Me.Go!" I yelled once more and then brought my knee up.

The man buckled and grabbed his manhood as he cursed.

"Why'd you knee my manhood?!" His voice was filled with pain.

I just straightened my shirt and huffed, "I said let go." I turned and started down the street. I didn't know where I was going or what I was going to do, but I knew I wasn't sticking around that post again.

Chapter 16

The mutt followed me a few blocks down from the last lamp post and sat with me once again. I leaned against the church sign outside of the park that I had made a point to never return to.

He whimpered and wagged his tail as he looked up at me with his puppy eyes. He was a mutt, that was for certain. But at that moment I felt like he was the only friend that I actually had. I had Anthony, but he would come and go. This mutt didn't even know me and he had stuck by me that long already.

I leaned down and patted his head and looked around. He had to have been getting hungry. The night was still dark and it started to sprinkle. Nothing would be open at that time, not even most gas stations.

He whimpered again and pawed at my old Adidas.

"What do you want, boy?" I asked and knelt down. He stuck both front paws in my lap and licked my face.

"I don't have any food," I scratched behind his ear. He whimpered and whined again. I supposed that was how a mother felt for a child she couldn't provide needs for. As odd as it may have sounded, I was for sure that mutt was kind of like my child. It depended on me. It looked to me for comfort it seemed.

I shook my head and made any weird thoughts disappear before I noticed a pair of headlights pull into the parking lot. I ignored them at first, assuming it was just two crazy teenagers about to get it on or something. I just waited for the vehicle to start shaking to cue my exit.

I waited 20 minutes and nothing. The vehicle killed its lights and a person got out.

"Hey," a feminine voice called out and walked toward me. I was sure I was going to get in trouble. Sure I wasn't doing anything wrong, but with the luck I was having that night, a person was liable to yell at me for getting dirt on the church sign.

As the person got closer, I recognized her. She was the woman from the convenience store.

Amy?

"What are you doing out here in the rain?" She asked.

"Standing," I huffed.

From what I could see of her face, she didn't appreciate my answer. She had to have been close to my age, maybe a little older. At least old enough to legally drive. "I don't need sass," she joked, "seriously, don't you have anywhere to stay?"

I shook my head and crossed my arms across my chest. Was she about to give me the pity offer?

I hated pity more than anything. You'd figure someone in my position wouldn't mind.

"Well listen, if y'all want—y'all can stay in the church. I have an extra key and the pastor more than welcomes people in. There's—"

I held my finger up, "Listen Amy, I don't need church pity when I'm standing in the rain. If it wasn't raining would I still be getting this offer?" Her expression changed as if she was somewhat baffled by my words.

"Thanks but no thanks." I pushed off of the sign and started to walk, her hot on my tail.

"I'm just trying to help, Michael."

"I know, but me and this mutt are doing just fine."

She glanced down at the ragged German Shepherd that happily walked by my side.

"He's yours?"

I nodded and spat in a puddle.

"He's beautiful. Got anything to feed him?"

I stopped in my tracks and looked over my shoulder, "No..."

"Well, come by the store tomorrow and I'll hook y'all up." She chirped.

"Once again, don't need pity from the religious."

"I'm not being religious—I'm being a genuinely good person."

She had me there. I shoved my hands in my pockets and sighed, "We'll be by."

I started to walk again before she spoke once again, and made me stop in my tracks. " Mutt is too scraggly of a name for him ya know...I think Gabe fits him."

My ears tingle at the name. It did fit him well. My old mutt would from then on be known as Gabe.

Chapter 17

I wanted to go after the officer and beat on him until he released Gabe. But I knew the only good that would come out of that is — well nothing. Not only would Gabe be locked up in his little puppy pound jail. But I would be locked up for assaulting an officer.

"Hey!" I heard someone shout from a vehicle on the curb as they sat their coffee in, what I assumed, a cup holder. They quickly exited the vehicle and started speed walking to the man. The Boy had brunette hair, broad shoulders and a tattoo on the left side of his neck. I couldn't make out what it was from where I was standing, but it made him look tough.

"That's my dog," he said as he started to reach for Gabe. The officer yanked him away, "No collar, no tag, no owner." The man repeated.

The brunette dude quickly snatched Gabe from the officer's arms and narrowed his eyes, "I said it was my dog."

The officer was about to argue but then held his tongue and huffed up as if he was trying to appear tough, or bigger than the broad shoulder man.

"Stop pushing your chest out like an insecure thirteen year old girl." The brunette Boy snapped, making the officer immediately stop.

Why does he have so much authority?

His dominant figure made me feel somewhat intimidated, yet it made me feel somewhat safe.

After a moment of awkward silence as I watched the two of them exchange dirty looks, the officer finally spat and then turned around and began heading the opposite direction.

I sighed in relief as the brunette man headed my way with Gabe still in his arms. "This little boy is yours?" He asked with a perked eyebrow. I nodded slightly, embarrassed by my appearance in front of such a nice boy.

He smiled and set Gabe down, "Might wanna get a collar for him or that douchebag will keep coming back to get 'em."

I bit my lip and nodded, "When I get the money I will."

He then looked me down from head to toe. I could feel his eyes examining my dirty clothes, matted hair and filthy face. I looked down at Gabe who wagged his tail happily and was grateful to still be with me.

"Here."

I looked up and saw his hand inches from me. He was holding a twenty in his hand. I looked at his face. His eyes were sincere, yet dark. He had a nose piercing—as well as an eyebrow one as well. I noticed his right ear was pierced, unlike his left. He was rather clean. I could feel my cheeks flush as I stared stupidly at him.

The corners of his mouth curled up slightly, "My arm is getting tired."

With that, I was snapped back into reality and heat gathered in my cheeks.

"Twenty? For a collar?" I asked with my own perked eyebrow.

He nodded, "I figured you could get him a collar, some food, and you some food or whatever you needed. Just take it."

His voice sounded slightly hostile in his last few words, but I didn't hesitate to take the twenty and shove it into my pocket.

"Thank you," I smiled softly at him.

His curled lips were back straight as he nodded, "Anytime street—"

Rat...

"-Boy."

My stomach dropped as he got back in his car and drove off.

He didn't call me a street rat.

My mind automatically assumed what he was going to say—just for it to be shut down.

But who was he?

Street Boy? I snickered. Cool.

Chapter 18

I walked down the street with the twenty rustling in my pocket. I found myself still thinking about The Mystery Guy. The way he just helped a stranger, not just any stranger either, a homeless one!

It amazed me how someone could just do that. It wasn't none of his business but he made it his business. The thought of him brought a smile to my mouth, which was somewhat rare.

I rounded a corner and pressed the bottom at a crosswalk light and watched as the numbers counted down for it to stop traffic.

Gabe painted happily by my side.

Street Boy.

My mind kept reverting back to the little name he called me. I don't know why I was so hooked on it. It made me feel somewhat special.

That car...

A black 2016 Mustang.

Why I remembered it, I don't know.

The hand signaled for me to walk across, so I scurried across. I was still carrying a bag that contained a safe keeping box in my right hand. Where was I gonna put it as I walked into Walmart?

I bit my lip and just continued to hold it as I walked in after walking a mile or two down the road after crossing the road.

The bright lights illuminated my somewhat dark skin. My eyes tried to adjust however it took a good while. I managed to run into three people in the process. I walked straight towards the back of the Well-sized store to the bathrooms. I didn't like using the ones in the front—too many people.

As I passed a worker, they stopped me and informed me of Gabe, who was still following me. I explained why I was there and what I was going to buy. To my surprise the woman told me she would hold

Gabe until I came back with a collar and leash. Another thing I have to get on my list. A leash.

I nodded and expressed my gratitude before hurrying to the bathrooms. My bladder was about to burst as I stormed through the doors into the empty bathroom. Thank God it was empty.

I went into a stall and immediately relieved myself. It was nice to be able to use a clean bathroom. A lot of times when you lived on the streets, you had to use portable toilets, AKA porta-potties. They'd be filthy and smell as if something had died. But it was either that or risk the humiliation and embarrassment of getting caught by a cop for indecent public display. Yeah, trying to take a crap on the streets.

I finished and did what I had to do.I placed the tissue in my worn out underwear. I probably should buy more.

But it was the last thing on my mind. Did I need more? Yes. But was I gonna die without it, no.

I finished up and left the stall. I washed my hands and while I was at it I washed my face and up to my elbows. The warm water felt wonderful on my dry, cold skin. I got my face mostly clean before drying off and slipping my bag on my arm and then I left.

I stopped by the pet section and picked up the cheapest collar and leash. Collar being $6 and the leash being $8.

Fourteen dollars. That leaves me with six dollars.

As I headed back to the worker my mind wondered what I could get with $6. What did I need? Underwear? No. They're not ripped, or falling apart. Just old. Perhaps a coat? Yeah, it would be getting colder. But would I be able to find a jacket that is $6.. most likely not.

I eliminated thought after thought until I landed on one. I could buy a blanket. That would be something I could really use and would provide some warmth.

I got back to the worker.

She looked at me, "I see you got the collar and leash." She smiled at me. I guess she was surprised I actually came back.

"Gabe's my baby," I said warmly, though it sounded a little odd.

"Gabe's his name?"

I nodded and handed her the money for the collar and leash after she scanned it with her belt scanner. I then began to remove the tags.

"He's a beautiful dog for sure. Find him on the streets?"

I nodded again and slipped the collar over Gabe's head and tightened it to fit. He was so thin it was hard to get it tight enough. I then clicked the leash onto the collar and stood.

"Can I ask a question?" The worker asked as she looked at me with a sympathetic look.

"Yes ma'am," I somehow managed to chirp.

"Why are you on the streets?"

I could tell she wasn't trying to offend me, or hurt my feelings. It was a common question I always got asked, so it became normal and my answer was always the same.

" Sometimes, kids aren't so fortunate." I gave her a forced smile and started to walk off again until she spoke again.

"Were you kicked out?"

Kicked out ?

I shook my head, "Let's just say... I'm better off in the streets." I left her with that and headed off to another section to retrieve a blanket.

I managed to find a blanket for $5.44 and it was a thin fleece material. Better than nothing I assumed. I checked out and headed back out into the cold.

Kicked out? Is that what that woman first assumed? Who could blame her.... but then again... who is to blame?

Chapter 19

I started to head back to my overly saturated box from the night before with Gabe on his brand new leash. I felt somewhat classy walking with Gabe on the bright blue leash in his dark teal collar. At least I could have something to show for.

Gabe just pranced by my side, not minding the leash that was hanging in front of his eyes. I wrapped some of the slack around my hand so he didn't have to have it dangling in front of his face. We started to pass the bus stop and I saw someone laying on the bench. I peeked and sure enough it was him.

"Mr. Lawson!" I chirped. He looked and leaned up with his nearly toothless grin, "Well hello Michael!" His voice was as enthusiastic as ever, "How are you doin'?"

I went and sat beside him and gave him a hug, "Doing pretty good for once!"

Gabe sat in front of us with his head tilted and his tongue hanging from his mouth. He pawed at Mr. Lawson's old worn out sandals as he barked.

Mr. Lawson chuckled, "That's great! And who's your little friend?"

"That's Gabe!"

"He's a beautiful breed—German Shepherd.. where did you find 'em?"

"He was outside of my box. Once he saw me, he wouldn't leave." I couldn't help but grin. Finally, someone who wouldn't leave.

"I guess that means y'all were meant for each other." He said as he patted my shoulder.

"I guess so!"

We both watched as cars drove by. Gabe laid down and I started to hear something. I looked at Mr. Lawson. He was holding his stomach and giving a look of discomfort. I peeked an eyebrow and glanced from his stomach and his face.

"Are you alright?"

He then noticed me halfway staring and stopped holding his stomach, "Oh! Of course. Just a little hungry, that's all."

I have never seen someone give such looks when hungry. But who knew the last time he had an actual meal.

Maybe...

Maybe Anthony could get him something!

I stood to my feet, "Come with me!" I grinned big and held out my hands. I really wanted to get back to my box. But. Mr. Lawson needed me.

"Where are we going?" He took my hands and I pulled him up and steadied him.

"I have a friend who can get you an actual meal," I gathered his raggedy bag of what looked like junk, but I knew it wasn't.

I made it a point to never openly assume something was trash just because it looked like it. Many think my box is trash—-but in actuality it's my home. Mr. Lawson's stuff may look like trash, but it's something different to him.

I slipped the bag over my shoulder and held his old, dry hand. He was getting up in age. I was surprised he had lasted that long on the street. But he's a warrior. That's what the streets make a person into if they truly wish to survive.

"A meal?" Both of his eyebrows perked up as if he hadn't heard the word 'meal' in decades. I nodded. "Yes sir. He helped me get a meal."

I slowly led him to the usual spot where the group met up everyday. We rounded the corner and there they were. I tried to scan the crowd for Anthony before we got too close, but I couldn't see him.

I glanced at Mr. Lawson, who was panting like Gabe from the walking we did. "Here, stay here and I'll go get my friend if he's there." He gave me a nod and I handed

Gabe's leash to him before I turned and headed toward the crowd.

Please be here Anthony.

I thought as I made my way through the stray people doing deals. I slowly enclosed the more dense part of the crowd where I saw Anthony dealing something.

Yes!

"Anthony!" I called out and waved my arms to grab his attention. After a minute or so, he told the crowd goodbye and came out of it to where I was standing at the time.

"Hey Michael, what's up?" He asked as he shoved a few KitKat bars into his pocket.

"I need a favor."

"What kind of favor?"

I hated to ask favors from anyone. It made me feel like I'm using them.

I looked back at Mr. Lawson and bit my lip, "My friend hasn't had an actual meal since—I don't know how long. Do you think you could—?"

"Grab him some grub?" He smiled at me.

I glanced at him and nodded, "He's really hungry. He looks like he's in pain."

"Come on.." he took my hand and started leading me back to Mr. Lawson.

I allowed him to drag me back to him and we stopped in front of them. "Hello, I'm Anthony."

Anthony gave him a warm smile and held out his hand for Mr. Lawson to shake.

Mr. Lawson took it and shook it.

"I'm James Lawson," Mr. Lawson said in a raspy voice.

"Are you hungry?"

I could tell Mr. Lawson was hesitating.

Yes, he's hungry. I think...

Mr. Lawson then nodded, "Yes-"

"Let's go get you something," Anthony took the leash from him and held onto it himself.

Mr. Lawson looked Anthony up and down, "Son, you don't have to do this. You're young, you use whatever privileges or such for yourself. Not on some old coot like me."

Anthony shook his head, "Family comes first." He protested.

Family?

Mr. Lawson looked as if he was about to cry at that point. Even I myself was getting tear filled eyes.

Family..... I like the sound of that. Is that what Anthony considered me as? Family?

My heart felt warm and a smile appeared on my face as I followed behind the two as they talked. Gabe hung back with me, given the slack from Anthony.

Anthony... Anthony is like a Younger. A good one, with a warm heart....

Chapter 20

We arrived at that fast food Chinese stand that Anthony had taken me to once before.

"Hey Rick!"

A moment later, Rick leaned out of the stands window opening and looked, "Well hey there Anthony! What's up my dude?"

"Nothing much, Hey—do you think you could hook my—"

"No man can do that."

My eyebrows shot up and I felt a sunken feeling in my stomach.

"Huh? Why?"

"Man, we are barely making profit as is. We can't just go around handing out free food. If I knew you were just going to bring your friends along I wouldn't have given you the free stuff either."

Anthony furrowed his brow, "fine.." His voice was deeper than usual and more hostile. He turned, "follow me."

Me and Mr. Lawson followed Anthony down the street a few blocks to an abandoned building. He crawled through a shattered window and told us to wait outside.

We waited for several minutes before he actually came out.

He was holding something green in his hands as he hopped through the window onto the pavement.

"Here," he held out what looked like $10.

Mr. Lawson looked at it and shook his head, and pushed Anthony's hand back to him.

Anthony looked at him as if he were crazy for turning it down.

"Sir, you need this. You can get yourself a decent meal. Maybe even two."

"You need that more than I do, son." He patted Anthony's shoulder and smiled, "You're young—you have a future to tend to. That money will help it if you allow it to. I—" he paused for a moment to cough. It sounded horrible.

"—I'm just making it day to day. I've already lived my life." He gave Anthony's shoulder one last Good pat before he bid us farewell.

I watched him as he walked away, and Anthony stood somewhat bewildered. "He didn't take it." Anthony finally spoke after minutes of silence.

I looked at him and sighed, " That's Mr. Lawson for you. He never receives, he only gives." I wished he would have accepted that money just that once. Maybe he could've gotten a good meal and some medicine for that cough.

"He's a good man, I must say." He put the money back into his pocket.

"I don't know what future he's talking about though," he shrugged and left his hands in his pockets.

I looked at him and perked an eyebrow.

"You're young, you still have a life ahead of you."

"Highly doubtful. I'd be lucky if I woke up tomorrow."

"'That may be true, but you have a better chance than he does."

Anthony gave me the utmost questionable look.

"Are you saying he's gonna die?"

I shook my head.

"No, I'm saying that he is old—you are young. He has seen better days. You're going to see better days."

That silenced Anthony. He probably wondered how I could be positive yet somewhat dark at the same time. He probably didn't like that I was making his chances sound better than Mr. Lawson's. But I knew Mr. Lawson probably had some health issues. It just came with aging.

Anthony and I are still young, we can fix what we're in and emerge from the twilight. I came to believe Mr. Lawson believes that he would never be able to get out of his situation. He was too old..

Too late.

Chapter 21

The night enclosed the streets fast. And I was by myself with Gabe once again. I went back to my box and sat outside of it as the sun fell behind the city buildings. It reminded me of the first night I spent on the streets. Oh the memories.

Gabe was asleep inside the box, and the temperature began to drop. I looked back at the box and it surprisingly dried throughout the day.

I sighed and stood to my feet and looked around before gathering my things that I had sat on the other side of the box earlier. I unwrapped the blanket and wrapped it around me as I climbed inside my box. I snuggled up to Gabe and wrapped my arm around his furry little body.

I fell asleep almost instantly. I slept until it was almost pitch black outside. Anywhere there wasn't a street light, it was a pitch black abyss. I was awoken by someone peeling out in the street. Making the tires squeal loudly. I emerged from my box to see the car still peeling out. I was utterly pissed off at that point.

Gabe peeked his head out as he barked and growled.

I tried to keep him in the box but he soon broke free and ran toward the car. I ran after him yelling out his name. He didn't stop, but just jumped on the side of the car. His claws left scratch marks all along the door and the car's ignition soon stopped humming and the door flung open.

I stopped and held my breath awaiting an angry driver to scream at Gabe and me.

I squinted and it was him...

The Mystery Guy

"Whoa Whoa!" he grabbed Gabe. Gabe tried gnawing and biting on the Boy, but he still had a lot of puppy teeth, thankfully.

"I'm so sorry!" I said as I rushed to the middle of the street.

The Mystery Guy looked back at his car and cursed, "Stupid —"

"Please don't hurt him! He was just annoyed and protecting me and—"

"Chill—Wait." He looked at me and the corners of his mouth curled up. His eyes lightened and he set Gabe on the ground. "Well if it isn't the Street boy ." He chuckled.

I looked down at the ground as my face grew red. He remembered me how he could forget we had been around the world together.

"How are ya?"

"I'm—"

How was I doing? I guess I could've told him great or horrible but I was neither. I was scraping by and surviving.

"—Decent."

"Just decent?" He raised his eyebrows and smirked. I picked Gabe up off the ground and held him as I coughed slightly.

"Yeah, ya know—making it."

"I gotcha. I see you got a collar." He smiled.

I nodded, "Yeah, thank you for giving me the money for it. Now I don't have to worry about someone trying to take him."

"No problem." He pulled out a box of cigarettes from his back pocket. I watched as he put it between his two full lips and lifted the lighter to it.

He perked an eyebrow, "What are you staring at?"

I didn't know you smoked? Lord help me..

He pursed his other eyebrow and smirked. He took a long drag and exhaled the smoke into the night sky. I couldn't help but watch as he looked up and exhaled it. The way he craned his neck and displayed his Adam's apple made my face even more red.

I looked back down at Gabe, who was just watching me with a goofy expression. I smiled and patted his head, "Yeah, you're grateful for your collar."

He wagged his tail and I felt The Mystery Guy's eyes on me once again.

"So, where do you stay?"

I glanced back at the alley where my box was. He glanced as well and hummed slightly.

"You live down there?" He nodded toward the alley.

I nodded, "Yes..." With all that was in me, I was hoping he wouldn't ask to see what I slept in.

"Can I see?"

Dang it.

I looked at him, embarrassment filled my body.

"I suppose."

A lot had seen where I lived before, so I figured it made no difference whether he saw it now or later. But I still couldn't push back the embarrassment I felt as I led him to it.

Chapter 22

After The Mystery Guy had seen my place he grew more sympathetic towards me. I didn't like it. I didn't want someone's sympathy for me because of what I lived in. It was my home. I didn't mind it.

The night grew cold. I shivered in my box next to Gabe. Even he was shaking in the cold. I found myself trying to warm my hands with my breath, but it was no use.

I soon gave up on sleeping. It had gotten so cold that I was concerned if I would wake up if I did fall asleep. I shivered even more once I sat up.

My thoughts began to wander. I remembered the kindness of Amy from the convenience store. I was such a jerk to her, and I started to regret it. She only wanted to help. I could have used a nice warm, soft pretzel right about then.

I could feel my mouth watering. It was so cold though, that it just made my lips even more chapped than they were.

I shrugged and pulled my knees to my chest and debated whether I should go and see if Amy was working. But every time I started to move I could feel the cold breeze sweep through. It made my hair stand on edge as I backed up against the back of the box, which was against the wall of the graffiti building.

I looked at Gabe and even he was starting to get a slight shiver. I frowned and placed my hand on his side, "I'm sorry boy." I knew I couldn't offer him anything better than my raggedy box. I even thought about just taking him to a shelter to save him from the colder weather that was to come.

I saw his tail wag slightly as he opened his brown eyes.

I bit my lip and decided to go ahead and try to go to the convenience store. Even though it was around 2am and 3am. I walked down the cold street with Gabe's pitter pattering paws beside me.

We walked a mile or two down the street and then I saw a rather sketchy man. He was dressed in a black tank along with a pair of jeans that rode below his hips. His skin was dark and was a contrast to his bright white shoes.

I crossed my arms across my chest and continued to walk. I glanced down at Gabe to make sure he was still beside me.

We started to pass when I saw the man perk his head up. "Hey!" He called out. I ignored him and kept walking.

Please don't try again.

I could feel my body getting more tense as I felt his eyes on me. What would he want with me?! I'm a dirt covered boy with matted hair. Not to mention my raggedy clothes and stench that followed me everywhere.

"Hey!" He said again and reached for my arm. I yanked it back and gave him a smug look in hopes of intimidation. "Oh you are a boy," he began to ramble about my facial features. How could he be so stupid.

I turned and continued to walk. I felt his eyes follow me. I wasn't about to let him sweet talk me into something. I knew what I was. I was a street rat with a dirty face.

It wasn't long after I started walking that I stopped.

What was this Boy going to do to me? Could I run? No, I couldn't even get out of his grip. I began to cower and I felt fear sink in.

"Just come with me sweet cheeks." He started trying to lead me into a different alley. Surprisingly it wasn't one that I was familiar with.

"No!" I yelled at him and tried fighting. He wouldn't let go and I was terrified. He was sure to rape me. I knew it. His voice grew harsh and eager. I hit and kicked him but it was no use. I tried biting but I just got slapped to the ground.

He grabbed me up and started walking again while he held my arm so tight that I knew it was bound to bruise.

"Let me go!" My voice sounded panicked and distressed.

I then heard a bark and patterning off my feet.

I looked and it was Gabe trying to attack the man. He gnawed and scratched at him, trying to get him to release me. The man kicked him aside and Gabe let out a yelp.

I watched as he could barely get up. Tears began to fill my eyes as I watched him manage to make it onto his paws.

My little hero...

I started to fight again only to be slapped down again. I wish he would have just left me down on the grime covered pavement. He yanked me up once again, this time by my hair. I yelped and tears streamed down my cheeks.

It made my face feel even more cold and my teeth began to chatter.

I slapped him but nothing was working.He finally got me into the alleyway and pushed me against the cold bricks of a building. It felt as if my face was going to freeze right to it. I struggled against his grip and tried to kick once again. But it was no use. He pushed himself against me and grabbed my chin with his hand.

It was then I could tell that his appearance was very much deceiving. He must be a low down scumbag to want to mess with me.

He probably even lived on the streets just like me. The only thing is I never harmed a fly.

"You should have just stopped and accepted my generous offer when I asked you nicely." He scoffed in my face.

"Let. Me. Go." I tried to sound strong and confident. But the truth was, I was a scared little mouse on the inside. The big cat had me pinned and what was I to do?

Please don't hurt me

My mind assumed the worst. I knew what he was bound to do and how it could get any worse if I gave him what he wanted.

No...

I pushed the lowdown compromising thoughts from my mind and struggled again.

He tightened his grip until someone shined a flashlight down the alleyway.

"Who's there?" The voice said. An echo down the alleyway and the man released me and ran. I slid down the wall with my knees to my chest. I began to cry for the first time in what seemed like forever.

I heard the footsteps draw closer and then someone knelt next to me.

"Are you Alright Michael ?" It was Larry.

I looked up at him and threw my arms around his necks and sobbed.

"Shh, it's okay. He didn't hurt you, did he?" Did he? I wasn't sure. My head still hurt and my back ached. But he didn't get what he wanted—that's all that mattered. I shook my head, "He didn't hurt me."

He sighed in relief and I let him go.

"You came just in time," I sighed.

He looked concerned. Just like a brother-like Boy should.

"I heard commotion and heard Gabe whimpering and saw him on the ground and I knew something was up."

"Gabe!" I hopped to my feet and ran down to where he was. He was still laying there.

He looked at me and yawned. "He'll be okay." Larry said to me as he crossed his arms.

"He's just as shook as you are."

I bit my lip and scratched behind Gabe's ear. It felt as if he and I were feeling the same pain.

"What if he comes back?" I asked.

"I'll stay here for the night in case he does." Larry replied as he sat against the front of the building.

I softly smiled and looked at him, "Thanks Larry."

"Hey, what are brothers for?"

He did act as if he were my brother. Despite everything he has been through and was going through, he still put others before him. He made sure people who were on the street had stuff to eat, and half decent clothes to wear. He sacrificed many of his free meals to others. And clothes he would find he would offer to others before claiming them for himself.

I never saw him be selfish. I never saw him take it when he wasn't in need. He was the definition of unselfish.

Chapter 23

Larry stayed the entire night next to me up against that building. He ended up giving me his big coat, leaving him in a long sleeve. He told me he was pretty much used to the chilling weather, however I still felt bad.

When the sun had risen, he set out to get his free meal from the Chinese cuisine stand. He offered it to me but I told him I wasn't hungry. Which was a lie.

I stood and Gabe was doing ten times better. He was up and walking as well.

I began to walk down the street as my lower abdominals decided to start hurting. I forgot my bag with the tylenol in it back at my box.

I reached the convenience store to find that Amy wasn't working. It was morning. She doesn't work mornings. Only at night. I shrugged and stopped outside of it. The exterior had been painted just a few months beforehand and now it looked good as new.

I looked at the 'Sales sales sales!' A sign that was hung in the window in big bright red and yellow lettering. Even it wasn't exciting to see. I turned my attention to a woman walking toward me, it was Amy.

"Hey!" I said with a smile.

She looked at me and then furrowed her brows before going into the store.

She just blew me off.

I furrowed my brows and started debating whether I should follow her in there, but I didn't. I stayed on the outside.

It wasn't long before she came back out and started to walk by me.

"Amy," I said. It seemed to have startled her.

"Oh, Michael." She looked up from her phone and at me.

"Do you think I could—"

"Get that pretzel from me?" She slipped her phone into her back pocket and crossed her arms, "tell me why in the living heck should I give you that when all you gave me was attitude when all I was trying to do is be nice?"

She had a point. I was a complete jerk to her. I didn't deserve the pretzel, much less her generosity.

I bit my lip and looked down at the ground. I was trying to contain my tears as the cold breeze brushed against my face.

It wasn't long before her hand appeared on my shoulder.

"Listen, I know it's tough on the street. And sometimes you just wanna say 'heck with it' and just forget being nice and stuff. But don't disrespect those who are trying to help you," she spoke softly despite the words she was saying, "there's a lot out there who would give a crap about you. But I do, and I want the best for you."

Her words seem to have hit me like a rock. It hurt but it was real, it was true.

I nodded as she finished and shuffled my feet before I spoke to myself.

"I'm sorry." I said humbly.

She gave me a warm smile and then put her arm around me, "I forgive you. But, you have to learn your lesson this time." She removed her arm and patted my shoulder before she walked off.

My heart sank as I stood there alone.

Wait...please I'm sorry. I'm hungry. Please wait.

She didn't wait, nor did she stop.

I learned that day that disrespect can be a very crumbling thing.

Chapter 24

I went back to my box and sat next to it and stared at the sky. Gabe sat beside me and licked my cheek from time to time.

I'm so hungry...

My stomach growled and my lips quivered. I was beginning to wonder whether it was from cold or hunger. You'd figure I would be resistant to hunger since many times I would go without food. But no. I got spoiled just those few times Larry or Mr. Lawson gave me something. Even Amy.

I wrapped my arms around myself and pressed my head against my knees. Another cold breeze blew by and I shivered. Gabe whimpered and laid down. His fur had started to thin. I think he was getting mange or something. It wasn't like I had money to go and blow on medicine for it either.

"Hey," a voice said. My eyes shot up and met Larrys.

"Hey." I said with a small voice.

"Whatcha doin'?" He asked and knelt beside me.

"Nothing," I shivered, "just trying to stay warm."

"Do you need my jacket?"

I shook my head and pulled my knees closer to my chest.

I wanted to feel the warmth of it, yes of course, but he needed it. And I, though cold and nearly freezing, couldn't bear to see him freeze.

He narrowed his eyes and sat beside me. His arm pressed up against mine.

"What's wrong?" I asked with that shiver in my voice. He turned his head to me and bit his lip.

"Michael," he said, "I need to tell you something." What was he going to tell me? Did he find a way to get free food for a lot of people? Did he help a granny cross the street?

"What is it?" I forced myself to say it through chattering teeth.

He looked up at the sky and then he turned his head toward me. I felt my heart jump slightly and I sighed.

His expression was straight and determined. He was serious.

"I'm going to die," he said as his voice cracked.

My heart felt as if it stopped mid-beat. It felt as if I was going to faint until he suddenly wrapped me in his arms..

I felt the tears stream from my face and I wanted to ask why, but I didn't. I couldn't. I just sat there. I don't know how ;ong time stood still in that moment but it did.

Chapter 25

I couldn't wrap my mind around the thought of Larry leaving. Loving, caring Larry. The one who had always been with me since I had been on the streets. The ones who helped me get food and warmth and even sometimes shelter!

I wanted to ask, but at the same time I didn't. He didn't like questions, but I needed answers.

"What do you mean?" I held onto him tightly.

After a minute, I released him and he looked into my eyes.

"I don't want to say, Michael." His voice was calm and smooth as usual. He always remained calm. "I don't want you to worry about when, or how. But—if I am not at the corner with the group everyday at three sharp, just know—I'm gone."

Why was he telling me that? I couldn't understand. Did he want me to be miserable?

Did he want to save me from having to worry about what happened to him? Why was he telling me? And yet—not telling me how.

"Michael, say something please."

I didn't realize I was distracted by my thoughts for a minute.

I bit my lip and crossed my arms across my chest. It hurt my heart. "Why?"

He perked an eyebrow at my question.

"Why are you going to die? Tell me, Larry."

"It isn't your concern," He said, "I just—am."

I know Larry always suffered from a terrible cough, and at times he would cough up blood. However, he thought I never saw it. He tried to hide it many times.

I don't know what was causing it though, and as I said before, he didn't like questions so I never asked.

"It is my concern, you're being secretive!" My voice was somewhat harsh.

"You're never secretive."

He looked down at the ground before he stood to his feet. I could feel the warmth generating from him leaving.

"Some things must be kept secret. You have secrets too I'm sure."

I did...

One big one too.

"No I don't," I lied, "I'll tell you everything."

"Michael, trust me this time. I love you like my big bro, but this is something you don't need to worry about."

He started to walk away until I pried myself from the concrete and grabbed his arm.

"Larry—"

He turned and looked at me.

I could feel tears welling up in my eyes as I tried to contain myself.

That was as vulnerable as I had ever been. He was my rock, my comfort and my strength. And he was going to leave. He's a part of me. How was I supposed to let that go?

"Please don't leave me," I whined. My voice was weak and cracking.

I saw sympathy in his eyes that were typically serious and indifferent. "Michael," his voice was calm and slightly shaken.

I could tell he saw the weakness in me; He took my hands in his and pulled me into another hug. His chin rested on my head. "Everything on this street fades away. Nothing is permanent. That includes people,." He said in a low, soft tone. It was comforting. I felt as vulnerable as an injured robin. I needed my strong eagle to stay by my side.

He was what kept me going.

"I can't lose you." I murmured from the crook of his neck.

He gave me a tight squeeze, "It's your turn to fly."

I stood there and watched as he walked away. Tears flowed from my eyes and I felt my head spin. My vision was blurred and my heart was broken.

He left me....

I felt overdramatic. I felt as if I was overreacting but I couldn't help it. What was once a stranger turned into a friend, a dear friend. And then I come to acceptance —and he leaves.

I bit my lip and brought a hand to my mouth as I tried not to just break down.

I couldn't and I wouldn't.

I had to be strong. There's no room for the weak on the streets and no time to waste tears. I would go to the corner street where the pity group meets and check for Larry everyday.

And the day he isn't there, I will know what happened, and at least I won't have to be left with worry, or questions.

I just wished I could have told him how I felt....

Chapter 26

I checked the group everyday for a week straight. He was there everyday and each time I laid eyes on him relief flowed throughout my body. Everyday that he was alive was a good day.

I waited at the bus stop with Mr. Lawson for about an hour before he spoke to me. He had been out of it lately. I feared that he may have been developing dementia of some sort. He somewhat had trouble remembering my name too.

"Good morning---Michael was it?"

I nodded and smiled, "Good morning Mr. Lawson. Staying warm?"

He was wrapped in a blanket, a red plaid one. He still wore a gray beanie on his head and hole filled gloves. I hardly understood the reason he wore them, it wasn't like they kept his hands warm.

"A little bit! If it gets any colder I may have to find myself a burrow to sleep in."

"For real!"

I shivered as the wind blew against us. The bus would be coming soon, but to my surprise the next vehicle that pulled up, wasn't the bus. It was a familiar vehicle. One that I had seen before.

"Hey Street Boy," It was him.

I smiled slightly and waved.

"What are you doing out in this cold?" He perked an eyebrow.

"I live out here--remember?"

He chuckled slightly and killed his car. He exited the vehicle and walked over to me after rounding the front of the car. Gabe growled and barked a few times before I popped his nose.

"Dang, he's grown," he said.

Gabe had grown significantly in such a short period of time. I was just happy he was still alive.

"Looks like he's been eating well too," he examined Gabe up and down. He patted his back a few times and then squeezed between me and the rail of the bench.

"What do you want?" I asked. It was unusual for someone to just randomly go and sit next to me.

"Just wondering how you've been. Haven't seen you around much."

Yeah, because I had been trying to find places to remain warm. But it wasn't like he would understand that. There he was driving a Ferrari and wearing Buckle clothing. He could have access to heat and meals anytime he wanted.

Meals...

I figured I would have to kiss meals goodbye and go back to small infrequent snacks.

"I've been here," I shrugged and slouched on the bench.

I felt his eyes on me and I felt somewhat uncomfortable. I stood to my feet, Mr. Lawson's was now on me.

" I have to go." I said and started walking off.

The Mystery Guy hopped to his feet and followed me just like Gabe. Well not exactly like Gabe.

"Wait," he grabbed my arm. I shot a look at him and he chuckled.

"Listen, I know what you're thinking," He said. I doubted he did.

"Most likely not."

"You think I am some creep who will give you a meal and place to stay in exchange just for sympathy ," He was dead on correct. It wouldn't be the first Boy to offer either. "However, you're wrong. One, I am not that person. Two, I wouldn't take advantage of someone in your situation--or in fact, anyone. That's wrong. And three, I am a nice Boy who wants to help you out, out of the kindness of his heart." He smiled at me warmly. I felt my cheeks flush until I shook my head and looked down at the ground.

I didn't need his help, all I needed was Larry. Larry was the only one who needed to help me.

"Come on," He took my hand, not forcefully, but gently. "I'll buy you some new clothes, I'll give you a place to stay, food to eat and the only thing I ask in return is that you try and pick yourself back up and maintain the things."

I tilted my head to the side, somewhat confused.

He sighed slightly, "I help you onto your feet--but you gotta promise me you'll walk when it comes time."

"Why are you doing this for me?"

"Because, you deserve better than this."

"Doesn't everyone?"

A look of surprise appeared on his face and it was as if I intrigued him. He smirked at me and shook his head slightly.

"Good point," He said, "But--"

There's always a but.

"I can only help one person at a time, and it just so happened to be you. Now come on, please."

He wasn't going to let me go. He was determined that he was going to give me a chance at redeeming myself I suppose.

"Okay..." I gave in. "Can Gabe come?"

He glanced down at Gabe, who was all eyes and tongue staring back up at him.

"Of course," he patted Gabe's head and led us back to the car.

To my surprise, Mr. Lawson was already asleep.

I climbed into the passenger seat of the car while he loaded Gabe into the back seat.

He circled the front and got in.

"Ready to go?"

I nodded and he drove us away..

Chapter 27

We spent the entire evening after that in silence. He showed me to the guest bedroom in which was simply--as he would say--divine as I prepared for my trip to florida. He left me alone there and went to bed by himself. Gabe was asleep at the foot of the bed as I stared up at the ceiling. It was weird laying on a soft, dry surface for the first time in 3 years.

I smiled, closed my eyes and thought about Larry. I was doing it for him. But I still felt guilt in my gut--which was very full. There was a television in that room too. Along with a small couch, coffee table, its own bathroom and a beautiful red-oak dresser. I observed every crevice of the room. I snuggled in with the blankets and felt the sheets. So soft and clean. My eyes grew heavy and before I knew it, I was waking up to the sunlight shining in my eyes through the sheer white curtains. The walls were also that grayish-blue color, but the floor was dark wood.

I set my feet down on the floor, it was cold. But, it wasn't near as cold as the streets sidewalks were. I stood and went into the kitchen and managed to find the glasses and then pour myself some water. It was crisp and clean and ran down my throat like silk. I wondered what Larry was doing right then. Was he searching for food? Was he sleeping? Was he missing me?

What killed me most about my confusing feelings toward him was he really going to die? I couldn't stand thinking about it, so I stopped and turned on the TV. I sat on the couch in the living room and grabbed a throw blanket off the back. It was surprisingly warmer outside. A good 45 degrees.

"Welcome to the Talk on this cold December morning," the news lady announced.

"This morning--" She went on talking about the current political issues and useless rambles of liberals. The show was obviously republican. I watched for a while and heard Gabe's nail click across the tiles and into the living room. He hopped on the couch and laid his head in my lap. I continued watching until The Mystery Guy came in.

He was already dressed. A dark suit with a gray tie, shiny, obviously freshly waxed, dress shoes, and a pen stuck into one of the chest pockets.

"Good morning, Street Boy." He said as he started making his coffee--well--started the Keurig to make his coffee.

Chapter 28

"Good morning," I turned around and pressed myself against the back cushion of the couch.

"Sleep well?"

"Best sleep I have gotten in awhile." I smiled.

"I'm glad. I figured, while I am at work" He pulled out his wallet and slapped down some money. "I figured you could go have some fun."

"I really don't need the money, sir." I sighed.

"You don't want it?"

"Nope."

"You're quite a Boy, you know that?" He chuckled and left the money where he slapped it down. "It's people like you who motivate me to help others."

"What do you mean?"

"What I mean is, you truly want help--not money. Even someone who isn't in your situation probably would have leaped at that money. Yet, you didn't. You're definitely not greedy."

I sat there, somewhat bewildered . I never had someone brag so much on me before. I guess, when you live on the street you learn that everything isn't about money. A meal meant more than money. Clothes meant more than money. A nice look from a man or woman in the upper social class--meant more than money.

"Thank you.." I simply said and looked back at the TV.

"You're welcome. I should be home around five this evening. I'm going to stop and grab a plane ticket for you on my way home." He fixed his sleeves and then grabbed his coffee. Watching him drink it black made me cringe.

"So then, if you're up for it, we can get you some decent clothes for your trip this evening."

"What if I didn't want to go?

"Believe me, you need to get away from this place maybe you will find something better in your travels"

He took a few more gulps and then sat the coffee mug down. "Well, I got to go.

The house phone is right there with my office number beside it. If you need me, just call. Okay?" I nodded in understanding and he left.

Chapter 29

I sat there for a good 30 more minutes before changing and going into the kitchen to search for breakfast.

I opened the fridge and it was like heaven. I could make anything I wanted.

Omelets, french toast, bagels, pancakes, toast...

Thousands of things filled my mind as I gazed at it.

I decided on scrambled eggs. I cracked like--5 eggs into a mixing bowl and did all the proper steps to make the best scrambled eggs.

20 minutes passed and I was back on the couch. Bored...

After a while I decided to get off my butt and go find something to do. He left me with $200. I decided to take it and go ahead and buy a suitcase . I already knew where to get it anyways, so I figured I could get a head start on it.

Chapter 30

I left the apartment complex with Gabe by my side on his leash. We walked down the street and I noticed that I was going to have to pass the trade group. I pulled the hood of my white puffy jacket onto my head in hopes to not attract attention to the fact that I was spruced up.

Some looked at me, but the majority didn't pay attention. I felt as if they were looking though. They knew Gabe. And

Gabe made his presence known. I passed them and I sighed.

I soon arrived at the store and got the suitcase. When I walked back out, I spotted Larry across the street.

He was sitting against a building. He looked miserable. I never saw him like that. He was always smiling. Was he always like that when he wasn't around someone? As much as I wanted to go over to him. I didn't. I bit my lip and started down the street again...

I returned to the apartment and sat on the couch. I cried and cried, and cried, and cried. I was sad because I missed Larry. But I was glad to be off the streets as well. I had a strike of confidence growing inside of myself. I have never been so proud of myself. I wanted to tell Larry so bad. He was so smart. Before I knew it, 5 came around.

Chapter 31

The Mystery Guy walked in, he wasn't holding a book because I told the woman at the store to tell him that I came in earlier. Well, I told her not to say my name... I wasn't going to tell him my name until he told me his.

He undid his tie and placed it on the countertop. He looked aggravated.

"Hey," I said as I pressed up against the arm cushion like a little kid.

"Hey, Street Boy." Even his voice sounded irritated.

"You okay?"

"Yeah, I'm fine."

He walked and sat on the couch. He wasn't fine.

"What'd you do today? Well, besides purchasing the book." He smiled slightly. Good. It wasn't the book that set him off.

"Just watch TV and do work in the book. I used your computer to teach myself some things---if that's alright."

"It's alright. I was kind of expecting you to use it eventually anyways." He sighed and slouched. Something was seriously bothering me.

"Tell me," I crossed my legs and faced him, "What's up with you?"

He rubbed his temples and then ran a hand through his hair. He was stressed. It was obvious, if he wasn't--he has something misleading body-language.

"Today at work, a bunch of sales fell through and now the business is at risk of failing. I have to try and think of something that would increase sales before it gets any worse."

"I'm sorry, I wish there was something I could do."

Chapter 32

"Don't worry about it. I'll just have to make a good advertisement and go handing out flyers."

"That sounds hard."

"Not really, more humiliating than anything."

"Believe me, that's not humiliating."

For a brief moment, he looked at me with a look that screamed apologies. I guess he thought I was offended. "If you want--I could do it." I exclaimed.

He raised his eyebrows at me and turned toward me.

"You're not a part of the company."

"Exactly," I began, "If people see that I am not a part of the company yet, I am advertising, it might draw them in." I smiled, "No offense, but people talk trash about you business folks. Having someone who works for the company recommending others to buy whatever they're selling--that's cliche and people view that as just money hungry."

"What are you suggesting?"

"Let me do it. I am part of the lowest of low social class." I looked down at my clothes, "I mean, and you're a kind-hearted businessman. People don't view businessmen as---kind. So, if you use me as a before and after thing it would show that this company cares for people."

"I think I will follow."

"What even is the company?"

Chapter 33

"Well, we say that we help people---like the stereotypical companies that say they do, we really don't. We turn down people who really do need help--" He continued to explain that they provide insurance and such for people who really need it, however, like many companies that claim this, they don't do anything but take the people's money and then turn them away.

"So people like me?" I questioned.

"I'm sorry---but yes. I feel awful for it. That's partially why I want to help people like you get back on their feet." His voice seemed like it was filled with guilt.

"That's screwed up..."

He looked at me, his eyes filled with tears. Why was he crying?

"I'm sorry. I really do want to help people. That's why I got with this company. They said they helped people, that's why I started to work there. I have nowhere else to go, so I stay." He paused, "But, they lied. And are still lying. That's why we're failing. People are catching on."

"Are you helping me because I need it, or because you need it?" I had to know. My heart felt like it stopped when I said the words.

"To help you! And me..." He was being honest, I respected that.

"But listen, what I'm doing for you--that's what I want the company I work for to do for others! Others like you!"

"So, you do want me to advertise."

"Yes," I knew it, "would you?"

"Only on one condition."

"What is it?"

"The company BETTER start doing what it's supposed to do. I know how it is to be living on the street, and I never even heard of ya'll---which is bad because I could have used it." My voice was harsh again.

"But to think that I would have scrapped and saved my money or even walked in empty handed and not gotten any help, that makes me sick! But if I get out there and advertise, so help me god, you better help ANYONE who goes into that building."

He looked intimidated but he smirked and sat straight, "I promise that the business will do its job right. Especially after this. Don't worry."

Chapter 34

I shrugged, "I don't know why your boss could be such a jerk that he could do that to all those poor people...It's time to turn that around."

He sat there for a while, silent. He stood to his feet and looked at me. I didn't realize that somehow time flew by and it was 8.

"I'm going to head to bed...Be up by seven tomorrow morning. We got a lot of work to do, partner." With that he walked out.I was touched by the man's repetition of "Thank yous."After an hour, we gathered about 5 new customers. I felt slightly proud of myself. I felt like a business man—although I didn't have a job

The Mystery Guy seemed thoroughly happy with me as well.

We went and got coffee and such at Starbucks and sat on the patio.

"You're a natural," he told me before he sipped his iced coffee. He must have been crazy to be drinking something of that nature in the weather we were in.

"Think so?" I perked an eyebrow and dipped my warm Frappuccino.

"Yeah, totally." He set his drink down, "Like, you're convincing and persuading and—"

"Honest, trustworthy—everything you're not?"

He choked up slightly, "Excuse me?"

"If you were any of those things this business wouldn't be going down the toilet."

"Street Boy, you don't know what you're talking about." He tried to sound as nice as he could, but I could still hear the harshness in his voice.

"No, I do. I may not have grown up in the business stuff. But I do know a solid foundation in anything is honesty and trust.

Without those two things, everything will fall apart," I took a deep breath, "You have motivation, and love for the company, but as I said—-if you don't have trust and honesty within the company and don't portray the company as so—its a lost cause and you're just asking for failure."

He was speechless and aggravated. I hoped I made sense. I regretted spouting off after the words left my lips.

He stayed silent for the longest time and I felt a lot of tension. We soon finished our drinks and we left.

Once we arrived at his house, he yawned and closed the door behind us.

He told me goodnight and headed straight to his room. I felt as if I made him furious. And I think I might have done so.

Chapter 35

After some time went by I moved to Florida to start a new life or whatever it was that I was starting. I moved into a homeless shelter that was more like a home than a shelter. My new job was vending papers that the shelter had made up sort of like its own newspaper. After a few weeks had gone by, I had gotten a hang of the vending jig. I went from barely any confidence to fill out the slogans and such. And now things were different.I was my own man in a place I felt at home and welcomed.

I went home that evening with a sense of accomplishment. The new life I was living was amazing....

ABOUT THE AUTHOR

Michael D White is the Author of a number of amazing new books.He was born in Texas and raised in California.

www.ingramcontent.com/pod-product-compliance
Lightning Source LLC
LaVergne TN
LVHW050531160826
845677LV00011B/1993

* 9 7 9 8 8 3 7 1 6 2 5 5 8 *